# BOREDOM BUSTERS

## By Cindy S. Hansen

Loveland, Colorado

# Boredom Busters

Copyright © 1990 by Cindy S. Hansen

**Fifth Printing, 1994**

**Credits**
Edited by Eugene C. Roehlkepartain
Designed by Judy Atwood Bienick

Scripture quotations are from the Holy Bible, New International Version. Copyright © 1973, 1978, 1984 International Bible Society. Used by permission of Zondervan Bible Publishers.

**Library of Congress Cataloging-in-Publication Data**
Hansen, Cindy S.
　　Boredom busters / by Cindy S. Hansen.
　　　　p.　cm.
　　ISBN 0-931529-77-8
　　1. Amusements.　2. Indoor games.　3. Youth—Recreation.
I. Title.
GV1201.H36　1990
793.7—dc20　　　　　　　　　　　　　　　　　　　　　89-78030
　　　　　　　　　　　　　　　　　　　　　　　　　　　　　CIP

Printed in the United States of America

# Dedication

*To Dan, my husband,*
*and*
*to my twins, Steve and Thom,*
*with whom there's never a dull moment.*

# Contents

## Part 2: Wild 'n' Wacky Boredom Busters

# Part 3: Race 'n' Relay Boredom Busters

# Am I Interrupting Something?

It's mid-meeting, and you've lost your kids' attention. Marcie is contemplating a crack in the ceiling. Dan is studying his shoelaces. Judy is staring at her watch like an eagle diving for a mouse. Tyrone is writing a note to Stephanie.

How do you pull these kids back into the meeting? Call the boredom busters!

*Boredom Busters* is filled with 84 creative, quick, simple-props-only, get-the-blood-circulating activities that get rid of the fidgets. Use these ideas to:

● add unexpected, involving breaks in meetings, retreats, special programs or classes;

● refocus kids' attention back to your meeting;

● recharge kids' enthusiasm;

● build friendships and group cohesiveness; and

● show kids church activities can be fun as well as faith-building.

## Questions About Interruptions

It may seem odd to interrupt a meeting on purpose. After all, we spend lots of time *getting rid of* interruptions. But boredom busters are different.

These interruptions are intentional breaks in a program's uniformity or continuity. They're like commercials in your program that help kids refocus and re-energize.

So what questions do you have?

**Why should I interrupt?** Sometimes you may think a program is flowing, but kids think it's stopped and clogged. Young people have short attention spans. It's tough to plan high-energy activities that keep kids focused. Kids need breaks and changes to stay interested. Boredom busters work wonders in helping them release energy so they can focus on the program.

Also, kids are exposed to colorful, exciting TV programs

and movies every day. If we want to compete for teenagers' attention, we need to continually hook and re-hook kids' interest.

**When do I interrupt?** Only you can know when to interrupt. Be tuned in to the atmosphere of your program. It's probably time to energize kids if you see or hear two or more of the following:

- eyes wandering or closed;
- blank looks in response to questions;
- kids slumped in chairs, leaning back, arms crossed in front;
- chattering or whispering; or
- fidgety movements.

**Won't kids lose their train of thought when I interrupt?** Yes. And that's the point. Use these when many kids' thoughts aren't focused on your topic. For the few who really are focused, an interruption just re-energizes them. Unlike many adults who have trouble shifting gears quickly, kids shift their energy constantly.

**How do I get kids to refocus on the program?** Simply state, "On with the show" or "Back to the program." You can briefly highlight main points covered so far, or ask kids to search their memories and state program highlights. The review reinforces what you've covered.

## Dos and Don'ts About Interruptions

When you interrupt, use these tips to keep your boredom busters from messing up your meeting.

**Be enthusiastic.** Let your enthusiasm spread. Interruptions should be lively and energizing—bright breathers to liven up a sleepy atmosphere.

**Keep transitions quick.** Get into and out of an interruption quickly. Don't spend a lot of time getting ready. In other words, be prepared. Know what interruption you want to use ahead of time.

**Lead energizing activities that don't put down anyone or make anyone feel inferior.** We're the children of God, so we should at all times "encourage one another and build each other up" (1 Thessalonians 5:11).

**Include everyone in the activities.** Keep your eyes roving for "hanger backers" who are reluctant to participate. Some kids are more shy than others and need a little extra coaxing to join in.

**Play games everyone can win.** Don't play games that affirm only the athletic or intellectual kids. All participants are affirmed when you play everyone's-a-winner games. And nobody feels like a failure.

**Encourage cooperation, problem-solving and teamwork.** We're called to work together as the body of Christ. Teamwork builds community and friendships.

Choose sides in an edifying way. Never divide into teams by having two captains each choose people to be on their team. This leaves the last-chosen few feeling horrible. Here are some ideas to divide into groups:

● Divide according to birthdays.

● Have kids repeat a theme for the day, one word at a time. For example, if your theme is "God loves you," have all "Gods" form a team, all "loves" form a team and all "yous" form a team.

● Make theme name tags. For example, if you're studying school survival skills, make several name tags in the shape of pencils, school buildings and books. Divide into groups by having kids find the others wearing their same name tags, or form smaller groups of three by having kids find two others wearing different name tags from their own—one pencil, one school building, one book.

**Adapt the activities to fit your group size.** All the activities in *Boredom Busters* can be used in a small group. If your youth group has more than 12 to 15 members, form more teams when necessary.

**Use and adapt the ideas to complement a retreat or meeting theme.** If you're studying the stoning of Stephen, play "Paper-Wad Dodge Ball" (page 62) to let the kids experience stoning. If your meeting theme is love, play "Musical Paper Plates" (page 46) using love songs in the background.

Forge ahead, youth leaders. Read and enjoy *Boredom Busters*. Use it to recharge your kids and add sparkle, energy and unexpected fun to your activities.

# Part 1

# Quick 'n' Easy Boredom Busters

# ⁑1⁂ Couple Connections

Say: **Turn to the person sitting closest to you. Tell that person one good thing that happened to you today.**

Then explain that you'll say various body parts for the partners to "connect." Try these connections:

- elbow to elbow;
- hand to neck;
- knee to knee; or
- foot to shoulder.

After a few connections say, **Couple combination change.**

Have kids each form a new connection with another person and tell the new partner their favorite thing to do on a Saturday morning. Then try other connections:

- ankle to ankle;
- toe to toe; or
- back to side.

As the final connection, say, **Seat to chair—and on we go with our program.**

# ⁑2⁂ Twin Hunt

Take advantage of kids' wandering eyes with this activity.

Say, **Look around the room and find a person with the same-color eyes as you.**

Have pairs each discuss one thing they like about the meeting so far. Have these people sit next to each other as you continue the meeting. Stop frequently during the remaining time and say, **Take 30 seconds to tell your twin one thing that stands out most for you from what you just heard.**

# 3 ✸ Oriental Rising

Get ants out of kids' pants by having them sit on the floor with their legs crossed and their arms crossed in front of them. Then have them try to stand up without using their arms.

After everyone is standing, have kids each bow to the person closest to them and say a warm "fortune-cookie" blessing such as, "God's blessings will shine on you" or "God will shower your days with sunshine because of your warm smile."

# 4 ✸ Quick Thinkers

(You'll need a wad of scrap paper.)

In the middle of a meeting when people aren't paying attention, toss a wad of scrap paper to someone and say, **(Name), think fast!**

Explain that the person has to catch the paper, then has three seconds to follow the same procedure and toss it to someone else. When the paper gets back to you, start the meeting again.

# ✸5✸ The Ears Have It

(You'll need a fresh ear of corn, some popcorn and two packs of sugarless gum.)

When you see your kids' attention wandering, draw them back to the meeting by saying: **And now, ladies and gentlemen . . . what you've all been waiting for . . . our awards ceremony for best listener and best participator. The award for best listener goes to . . .**

Announce the name of the person who has listened well for the first part of the meeting. Encourage the kids to clap and cheer as the award winner walks to you and receives his or her award—an ear of corn. Say, **This corn will ensure that you'll be all "ears" so you can listen and hear.**

Then continue. Say, **And last—but certainly not least—the award for best participator goes to . . .** Announce the name of someone who has participated well. Encourage cheers and give the award winner a pack of sugarless gum. Say, **This gum will exercise your jaws so you'll be assured of quality participation in future discussions.**

Go back to the meeting and continue using positive reinforcement. Occasionally toss popcorn to those who are listening, or a piece of gum to those who participate.

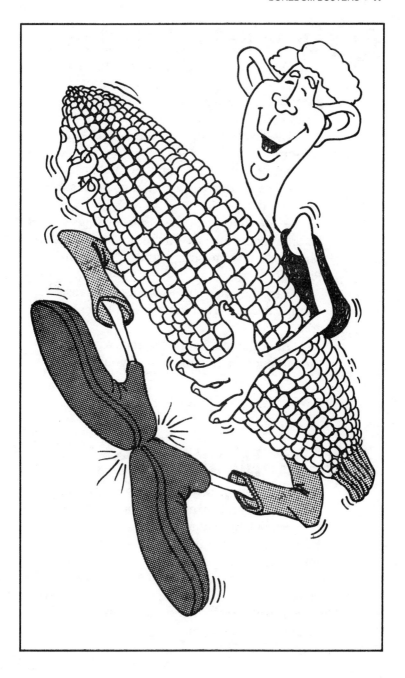

# 6 Organized Orchestra

Tell kids you're going to give them a chance to "shout with joy to God, all the earth! Sing the glory of his name; make his praise glorious" (Psalm 66:1).

Divide the group into three "orchestra sections."

● The first section claps in rhythm.

● The second section stomps percussion on the floor double time.

● The third section whistles or sings a favorite hymn such as "Joyful, Joyful, We Adore Thee" or a favorite song such as "Pharoah-Pharoah."

Vary the orchestra's volume—increase volume to loud. Then decrease volume to very soft.

After the marvelous concert, whisper it's time to continue the melody of your meeting.

# 7 Two-Minute Aerobics

Say: **Everybody up. Get your blood circulating and mind functioning again.**

Have kids run in place and do jumping jacks, head rolls and shoulder shrugs. Let kids take turns leading exercises.

As a last exercise, have kids sit down and stand up 10 times. Finally, have them sit down, take a deep breath, let it out and sigh, "Ah-h." Continue your program.

# ☀8☀Public Opinion Polls

(You'll need refreshments.)

Interrupt your meeting to take a public opinion poll. Make the room a continuum from one wall to the other. Ask agree/disagree questions from your study. Let young people discuss their opinions with people standing near them.

For example, if you're studying King David say, "All those who think God was too tough on David, stand close to the left wall; all those who think he was too easy, stand close to the right wall; all others stand in between, depending on your opinion."

Get back to the meeting by saying: **All those who want to complete the meeting so they can eat refreshments stand to the left; all who don't want to continue, stand to the right; all others stand in between.**

When everyone congregates to the left side of the room, finish your program and eat the goodies.

# ☀9☀One-Two Beat

Start a one-two beat by slapping your hands on your thighs then clapping. Have kids follow you. Then do this rhythmic-repeating chant. Say each line and have kids repeat it—while keeping the clapping-slapping, one-two beat:

**God**
**God is**
**God is great**
**God is good**
**Jesus**
**Jesus loves us**
**He forgives us**
**He's our Savior**
**Amen**
**Oh, yeah-h!**
Get back to the meeting with this chant:
**Now it**
**is time**
**to get**
**back to**
**our great**
**meeting!**

# ⭐10⭐ Noah Knows

(You'll need a Bible.)

Assign everyone a part to play in the Noah story using the following assignments:

● Ark—Several kids sing, "Sailing, sailing, over the ocean blue."

● Noah—One person stands up, waves his right hand and says, "I'm Noah."

● Wind—Several kids sway from left to right and say, "Whoosh-sh-sh-sh."

● Rain—Several kids clap their hands to make raindrop sounds.

● Waters—Several kids stomp their feet.

• Dove—One person flaps his or her arms and softly says, "Coo coo."

When kids all understand their parts, read aloud the Noah story in Genesis 8:1-12. Every time their word is said, have kids respond according to their assignments.

# ⚹11⚹ Try Not to Yawn

Ask two kids to come to the front. Tell everyone you're going to have a contest. Have the two people yawn and stretch as much as possible—trying to get the others to yawn. (Everyone knows yawns are catching!) Have others watch them and try not to yawn.

As people break down and yawn, have them join the yawners at the front. After a minute or so, have everyone stretch, yawn, open and shut eyes, and roll and shrug shoulders. Then get back to the meeting.

# ⚹12⚹ There's Good News and Bad News

(You'll need refreshments.)

Take a moment to refresh kids' memories about Creation by creating a good news/bad news story. Start out with a good news/bad news example, then let kids add their own. Be sure to end on a "good news" bit of information.

Here's an example:

**The *good news* is that God created the world out of a void and everything was good.**

**The *bad news* is the serpent.**

**The *good news* is that God made the Garden and Adam and Eve.**

Let kids continue adding other good news and bad news.

End with:

**The *good news* is you've done a good job creating a good news/bad news story.**

**The *bad news* is we have to quit our storytelling time.**

**The *good news* is you'll learn more things and you'll get to eat refreshments at the end.**

# ✳13✳ A Word From Our Sponsor

(You'll need a candle and match.)

Say: **And now a word from our sponsor. Follow me for an important commercial break.**

Gather in a dark closet or room. Light a candle and say: **Jesus is the light in the darkness. Trust him to guide you. Trust me to guide you back for the rest of the program.**

Blow out the candle and go back for more!

# ⭐14⭐ Scripture Scramble

(You'll need to prepare 3x5 cards as described in the activity.)

Write each phrase of a familiar Bible passage on a separate 3x5 card. For example, divide Psalm 23 like this:

- The Lord is my shepherd,
- I shall not be in want.
- He makes me lie down in green pastures,
- he leads me beside quiet waters,
- he restores my soul.
- He leads me in paths of righteousness for his name's sake.
- Even though I walk through the valley of the shadow of death,
- I will fear no evil,
- for you are with me;
- your rod and your staff,
- they comfort me.
- You prepare a table before me in the presence of my enemies.
- You anoint my head with oil;
- my cup overflows.
- Surely goodness and love will follow me all the days of my life,
- and I will dwell in the house of the Lord forever.

Mix the cards. Give kids each a card, and have them find other parts of the passage and arrange them in order. If you have more kids than cards, give one to each pair, or make more than one set. Read the cards when young people think they have them in order. Then read the Psalm from the Bible to double-check.

# 15 Back Rub

Form a circle with everyone facing clockwise. Say: **Everybody stand up and put your arms in front of you. Can you reach someone's back? If so, rub it!**

Give kids time to rub. Then say: **Turn to the right. Reach a back and rub it.**

Pause.

Say: **Turn to the right again. Reach a back and rub it.**

Pause.

Say: **Turn to the right again. Reach a back and rub it.**

Try scratching the backs, then patting them. Say: **Pat yourself on the back for a job well-done. And "back" we go to the meeting.**

# 16 Eat and Be Energized

(Fill a sack with inexpensive goodies such as candy, gum or fruit. Have at least one item per person.)

Say, **Time to interrupt our meeting for an energizer.**

Pass around the snack sack and let everyone grab something and eat it. Say: **Eat the snack and be energized. Here we go—on with the show.**

Keep the meeting going as they snack.

If you want to be more wild, simply toss the snacks to the young people and say, **Eat and be energized!**

# 17 A Balloon Feat

Give everyone an inflated balloon. Have young people stand in a close circle facing clockwise. Then have them place their balloons in front of their chests or stomachs. Have the kids scoot closer so the balloons are wedged between them and remain in place without using hands. Have them each place their hands on the next person's shoulders. Sing a song about Christian love as kids walk in a clockwise direction, keeping the balloons in place.

After the song, have kids shout, "We are loved." Squeeze until all the balloons are popped. Then on with the meeting!

# 18 I Know That!

Tell the kids that every now and then when you stop and ask, **Did you know that?** they're to stand up and shout, "I knew that!" Then, whenever you sense kids may be losing concentration, ask, **Did you know that?**

# 19 Twosome Tongue Twisters

Take time out to do tough tongue twisters. Have young people pair up with someone they're sitting by and create a tongue twister about the topic being studied.

A tongue twister on peer pressure could be "Peer pressure pounds people practically every school period." Have pairs each say their tongue twister and let others say it too. Then have them try it fast, three times in a row.

Focus kids' attention back to the topic with this tongue twister: **Time to tune back to today's topic.**

# 20 Do You Know Your Neighbor?

Say: **Find someone on the opposite side of the room to be your partner. Talk to each other for one minute and find out things such as favorite hobbies, food, music, movies or books. When I call time, I'm going to see how well you know your neighbor.**

When time's up, have pairs sit back to back and—instead of asking kids what facts they learned—ask:

- **What color shirt is your partner wearing?**
- **What kind of shoes does your partner have on?**
- **What color eyes does your partner have?**

See how observant kids were while they talked.

Then say, **Let's get back to the study and observe more amazing facts.**

# ⚡21⚡ The Answer Is . . .

(You'll need a piece of paper and a pencil
for every two people, new pencils to give as
awards, and refreshments.)

Announce, **It's time for a riddle break.**

Give every two people a piece of paper and
a pencil. Say: **I'm going to give your brains a
little exercise to wake them up. As partners,
you have three minutes to think of questions
that can be answered with "God." For
example, "Who made us?" or "Who was here
before anything else was?" or "Who is three
in one?" After three minutes, we'll read all
the questions. The team that writes the most
questions will get a prize.**

Call time, read the questions, then award the
most prolific question-creators a pencil. Say: **I
have another riddle for you. What's waiting
for us to finish and when we finish it we'll
get refreshments?**

Wait for someone to say, "The meeting."
Then continue where you left off.

# ⚡22⚡ Indoor Rainstorm

(You'll need two or three toy water pistols.)

Keep your meeting from becoming a
washout by using this interruption.

Have your group sit in chairs in a circle.
Point to one person and have that person snap
his or her fingers. As you rotate around the circle,

have other kids join in the snapping when you point to them until the whole group is snapping fingers. This way the snapping will get louder and louder. Have kids keep snapping until you point to them again.

Then starting with the first person, clap. Rotate around the circle again, having people switch from snapping to clapping as you point to them.

Next pat your thighs, and have the same person start this action. Continue around the circle. Then follow the same procedure with stomping your feet. This is the peak of your "thunderstorm."

Add excitement to the rainstorm by having an adult sponsor flick the lights off and on, and other leaders squirt water pistols into the circle during the stomping.

Now reverse the process. Turning in the opposite direction, have kids pat their thighs, then clap their hands, then snap their fingers. Then, one by one, have them stop.

Say, **Now that the storm's over, we can get back to our meeting.**

# ✼23✼ Can You Guess?

Play a guessing game to stimulate kids' brains. Have one person think of an action word such as "swim." Then have the others take turns asking yes or no questions to help them guess the word. Questioners must substitute the name of your church in place of the action word they're trying to guess.

Here's an example using the church name "Faith":

"Can you 'Faith' on roller skates?"

"No. You can't 'Faith' on roller skates."

"Can you 'Faith' in a swimming pool?"

"Yes. You can 'Faith' in a swimming pool."

"Is 'Faith' the word 'swim'?"

"Yes!"

The person who guesses correctly gets to think of an action word, and the game continues. Then ask if you can take a turn, and use this action word: learn. When a person guesses the verb, say, **Now it's time to continue our meeting as we learn new things.**

# ⟨24⟩ Chinese Fire Drill

When you want to get the adrenalin flowing, shout: **Chinese Fire Drill!** Tell everyone to jump up and start running clockwise around the room. When you say, **The light's green, time to get started again,** have kids run back to their seats and sit down.

# 25 Orange You Glad?

(You'll need several oranges.)

Peel an orange in front of everybody. Take your time and enjoy it. Toss out oranges to people to share. As they peel and eat, ask them to complete these thoughts:

- Oranges smell like . . .
- Oranges taste like . . .
- I'd rather eat an orange than a . . .
- When I eat an orange it sounds like . . .

Let kids form pairs and create their own knock-knock jokes using the word "orange." For example:

Knock, knock.

Who's there?

Orange.

Orange who?

Orange you wondering what kind of knock-knock jokes you can make?

Have the kids tell their knock-knock jokes. Get back to the meeting with this one:

**Knock, knock.**

**Who's there?**

**Orange.**

**Orange who?**

**Orange you glad we're getting back to our meeting?**

# ✺26✺ Getting Back on Our Feet

(You'll need masking tape.)

Without saying a word, walk to a large, clear area and tape to the floor a long piece of masking tape. Say: **Now it's time to test your perseverance—your ability to try again. Come over here and place your toes on this line.**

Have kids gather at the line.

Say: **Now fold your arms. The object is to kneel down and get back up without moving your feet or using your hands. Go.**

After everyone has tried the feat a few times, say: **Some situations we face are tough. But God helps us make it. He helps us get back on our feet.**

Have kids try the exercise again.

Then lead everyone back, and continue the meeting.

# 27 Interview Time

Ask kids to find someone as far across the meeting area from them as possible to be their partner. After partners find each other, have them interview each other with these three questions:

● What do you like best about this meeting so far?

● What'll you remember for the rest of the week?

● What would you tell a friend to get him or her to come to a meeting?

Have kids share their answers. Then ask, **How do you feel about getting on with the meeting?**

# 28 ABC Descriptions

(You'll need newsprint and a marker.)

Sit in a circle, and have kids think of adjectives that positively describe your church. Have the first person say an adjective that starts with an "A" such as, "This church is an **a**ctive church." The next person must choose an adjective that starts with a "B" such as, "This is a **b**eautiful church." List all the adjectives in order on newsprint. Continue until you've used adjectives from the whole alphabet.

Title your list "The ABC's of Our Great Church," and publish it in your church bulletin or newsletter.

# ☼29☼ True Identity

Before starting this game, make sure group members know everyone's name. This game will cement the names even more securely in their minds.

Choose one person to be "It." Have "It" hide his or her eyes. Then point to someone else and have that person say, "Hi, there. Isn't this a great meeting?" "It" then tries to guess who the speaker is. If "It" can't guess the first time, he or she can ask, "What do you like best about this meeting so far?" If "It" guesses correctly, have everyone cheer. If "It" can't guess the speaker's identity after hearing the answer, show the true identity by having "It" open his or her eyes.

Let the speaker then be "It." Then let a lot of people take turns being "It."

Read John 10:27-28: **My sheep listen to my voice; I know them, and they follow me. I give them eternal life, and they shall never perish; no one can snatch them out of my hand.**

Talk about how it was difficult to recognize people's voices. But remind kids there's one voice we know: our Shepherd's. Get back to the meeting and learn more about listening to and following the Good Shepherd.

# ✦30✦ Trivia Time

(You'll need a pencil and several 3x5 cards
for every two people.)

Announce it's time for a trivia break. Tell
kids they get to write trivia questions about what
they've just been studying. Pass a pencil and
several 3x5 cards to every two people. Have
partners think of questions and write one
question per card.

Divide the group in half and have teams
take turns asking the other team questions.
Teams win a point for every correct answer.

# Part 2

# Wild 'n'
# Wacky
# Boredom
# Busters

# 31 Sense Stop

(You'll need a blindfold, pair of gloves and refreshments.)

Say: **I "sense" we need a break right now. Let's play a game that shows how important our senses are.**

Gather everyone in a circle, and choose one person to stand in the center. Put the blindfold and gloves on him or her. When the blindfolded person says, "Go," have all the other kids walk clockwise in the circle. When he or she says, "Stop," have everyone stop. Then have the blindfolded person walk up to anyone and feel his or her face to try to identify the person. The person can't back away, but he or she can bend his or her knees to disguise height.

If the blindfolded person guesses correctly, have him or her take off the blindfold and gloves and give them to the "discovered" person to resume the activity. If the blindfolded person doesn't guess correctly, have him or her try one more time to guess the identity of another person.

Let everyone use the senses of tasting, smelling and hearing as they munch on refreshments and participate in the rest of the meeting.

# ⟨32⟩ Paper Airplane Messages

(You'll need a piece of paper and a pencil for each person.)

Interrupt the daydreamers and say, **Since your imaginations are flying away, let's make use of your imaginations with some high-flying advice.**

Give each person a piece of paper and a pencil. Have kids write a bit of advice they'd like to give others. For example, "Remember to start your day with a prayer" or "Don't forget to smile."

While kids are writing their advice, write this advice on a piece of paper: "Listen to and participate in the rest of the meeting. You'll learn more about God's will for your life."

Have kids fold the papers into airplanes and fly them for a while. Make an airplane of your paper, but hold on to yours for later. Then have participants catch an airplane that's not theirs. Take turns reading the high-flying advice.

Read the airplane you prepared as a last bit of advice. Then follow that advice!

# ✳33✳ To See or Not to See

(You'll need carrot sticks, a Bible, a bottle of eye drops and refreshments such as carrot cake or carrot juice.)

Ask kids to stand along the walls in the meeting room. Make sure kids are along all four walls. Say: **Close your eyes. Imagine you've completely lost your sight. Your goal is to reach the other side of the room without running into anyone. You must rely on your other senses to avoid collisions. We'll stop when everyone has reached his or her destination.**

After all the kids have reached the opposite wall, ask them to open their eyes and sit down. Give each one a carrot stick to munch on while you read about Jesus healing the blind man in Matthew 9:27-31. Say: **An old saying is that carrots are good for your eyesight. So is Jesus. Jesus heals the blind. He helps us to see the way we are to live and treat each other. Let's participate in the rest of the meeting and "see" what other things Jesus has to teach us.**

Award a bottle of eye drops to a young person with the best "insight" to your study. Then serve sight-saving refreshments such as carrot cake or carrot juice after the meeting.

# ☀34☀ Get-to-Know-You Rotation

(You'll need music.)

Ask guys to stand up and form a circle. Next have girls stand up and form a circle around them. If you have lots more guys than girls or vice versa, form two circles by counting off in twos. Say: **I'm going to play some music. While the music plays, guys will walk clockwise, girls will walk counterclockwise. When the music stops, face the person opposite you in the other circle. If there's an odd number, form a trio. I'll ask a question and you'll discuss it with your partner. When the music starts again, start walking. We'll continue this process for several questions.**

Make up your own questions, use questions from *Talk Triggers* (Family Tree) or use the following questions:

● **What do you think of the meeting so far?**

● **If someone offered you $1,000 to start a bad rumor about your best friend, would you do it? Why or why not?**

● **If a classmate asked you why you go to church, what would you tell him or her?**

● **If Jesus came to visit you for a day, what would you plan to show him and have him do?**

● **If you could have a full day to do anything you wanted and if you had all the money you needed, what would you do?**

# ✳35✳ Musical Paper Plates

(You'll need a paper plate for each person except one, and some music.)

Say: **Get up, stand up and move around. It's paper-plate-pushing time.**

Distribute the paper plates. One person won't get one. Have kids place the paper plates in a large circle on the floor.

Give these instructions: **We're going to play a variation of Musical Chairs called Musical Paper Plates. Walk clockwise around the circle while the music is playing. When the music stops, sit on a plate. If you don't get a plate, you're not out. Instead, sit on the lap of a person who's sitting on a plate.**

Remove a plate for each time you stop the music. The kids are never out, they just keep piling up on the remaining plates and people. Continue until everyone is piled up on one plate.

Play the music one more time. Ask kids to go back to the meeting area, and sit down when the music stops. Start the meeting where you left off.

# 36 Crisscross Caper Tag

Play this game to illustrate how Christ has diverted all our sins onto himself.

Choose one person to be "It." Have "It" call the name of another person and chase him or her. Sometime during the chase, have other kids cross between the two and distract "It's" attention. "It" must then chase the distracter instead. If "It" ever tags the person, the tagged one becomes "It" and calls out a name of someone else to chase.

Keep playing and encouraging kids to divert attention onto themselves, just as Christ took our sins on himself.

# 37 Shouldered Out

(You'll need masking tape.)

Use masking tape to form a circle on a carpeted floor. Ask kids each to stand inside the circle with their arms crossed over their chest. The object is to "shoulder" people out of the circle. Anyone who crosses out of the circle is out; anyone who falls is out; anyone whose arms unfold is out. Have kids who are out, sit outside the circle and watch.

Afterward, talk about how this game illustrates cliques. Certain people don't want others in their group and give them the cold shoulder. You're "in" for only a short while until you get bumped out by someone else.

Ask the last person left in the circle to pull another in, who pulls another in. Continue until everyone's inside the circle again. Ask God for forgiveness when we shoulder people out of our lives. And pray that he'll help your group be warm and open to everybody.

# ✸38✸ The Mystery Word Is . . .

(You'll need a chalkboard, piece of chalk and eraser.)

Play this version of the old word game, Hangman. Think of a word from the lesson you're teaching; for example, servanthood. Place 11 blanks on the chalkboard—one blank for each letter. Tell the kids they'll raise their hands when they want to guess a letter of the mystery word. Tell them the word is from your study.

If the kids correctly guess a letter, fill it in the blank or blanks. If they miss, draw part of a person on the board using the following plan:

- First mistake: Draw a head.
- Second mistake: Draw a body.
- Third mistake: Draw a right leg.
- Fourth mistake: Draw a left leg.
- Fifth mistake: Draw a right arm.
- Sixth mistake: Draw a left arm.
- Seventh mistake: Draw a right eye.
- Eighth mistake: Draw a left eye.
- Ninth mistake: Draw a nose.
- Tenth mistake: Draw a mouth.
- Eleventh mistake: Draw a thought bubble.
- Twelfth mistake: Draw a light bulb.

Kids have 12 chances to guess the word. If they still haven't guessed by the time the chalk person is complete, tell them the word. Let kids try it a few times using other words from the study.

When you're ready to get back to the meeting, draw a completed person and say: **This person has a good idea. It's time to get back to the meeting and learn more.**

# ❋39❋ Hula-Hoop Toss

(You'll need lots of scrap paper, a Hula-Hoop and a trash can.)

Start tossing wads of scrap paper to unsuspecting kids to get their attention. Next, hand out all the scrap paper and have kids make paper wads for themselves. Tell them to hold on to the paper because they'll soon see a rolling target to toss the wads through.

Roll a Hula-Hoop across the front of the room. Encourage kids to toss their paper through the rolling target. Roll the hoop again, and let kids have another chance at the rolling target. Have kids keep count of how many times they make it through the hoop. Award the person who tosses through the most hoops the job of holding the trash can, and award the others the job of throwing in the wads of paper from the floor.

Use the trash can of wadded scraps as an object lesson. Say: **Sometimes we have days when we feel like wadded scraps of paper in a trash can. Crumpled, not worth anything, useless, no one misses us.**

Hold up the hoop.

Say: **But God makes us whole. His never-ending circle of love makes us worthwhile. We are his children.**

# 40 Break Out

Lead everyone to a carpeted or grassy area. Form one large circle, and choose one person to be in the center. Ask the circle members to clasp arms, and have the player in the middle try to get out. If he or she breaks out of the circle, have him or her run clockwise around the circle. Have the two people who the middle person broke through chase him or her. Whoever doesn't tag the person is the next to be in the center.

Step up the action with two kids in the middle trying to break through.

Also try changing the locomotion. After a center person breaks through, he or she can run backward, hop or skip. His or her chasers must do the same action as they try to catch the middle person. After you've let everyone run off excess energy, have them run backward, hop or skip to the meeting.

# 41 Jump-Rope Jingles

(You'll need several jump ropes, pieces of paper and pencils.)

Go to a large room or playground. Toss out several jump ropes, and ask kids each to grab one. All the kids holding one rope form a team. Say: **Each team is going to make up a new jump-rope jingle about church life. We'll also take time to jump around and get the blood circulating again.**

Here's an example of a new jingle. Instead

of "Cinderella, dressed in yella, went upstairs to kiss her fella. Made a mistake and kissed a snake, how many doctors did it take?" You could say, "Sunday school teacher and the preacher, went to church every Sunday and Easter..."

Pass out paper and pencils. Allow several minutes for creative brainstorming.

Have teams each teach their jingle to the rest of the group, and have all teams jump each jingle. Then have kids jump back to their seats and go on with the meeting.

# 42 Fashion Statements

(You'll need newspaper and a roll of masking tape for every three people.)

Stop what you're doing and give newspaper and masking tape to every three people. Tell them it's time to take a break. Give the trios five minutes to design a typical Sunday school student. They can only use the supplies you gave them to dress one member of their trio. For example, a trio could dress someone in a newspaper cape (super student) and a paper crown (child of the King).

After five minutes, have a fashion show. Ask trios to choose a person to be the emcee and describe the fashion.

At the end of the show say: **We're all models of God's Word. Let's learn more about him.**

Then on with your program.

# ✲43✲ Build a Body

(You'll need large marshmallows, miniature marshmallows, toothpicks and a Bible.)

Stop your meeting and ask a few review questions. Toss a marshmallow to each person who answers. Then say, **We'll take a marshmallow break and make a unique symbol of a Bible passage.**

Divide into groups by having kids alternate saying "build" or "a" or "body." All "builds" form one group, and so on. If you have more than 20 kids, just form groups of six to eight. Give each group a handful of large marshmallows, a handful of miniature marshmallows and several toothpicks.

Tell each team to build a body out of those supplies while you slowly read 1 Corinthians 12:12-26. All team members must participate as a group to build the body, and no talking is allowed.

After you've read the passage and teams have shown their marshmallow bodies, form a large circle around the marshmallow munchkins. Pray: **God, help us remember each one of us is needed. We're all a part of the body of Christ. Amen.**

Continue your study as kids munch on the extra marshmallows.

# ✸44✸ Telephone Interruption

(Arrange to have someone call you on a telephone halfway through your program. You'll need soft drinks and several hero sandwiches with lots of meat, cheese, lettuce, onions— enough so everyone can have a good portion.)

Tell kids at the beginning of the meeting you're expecting a phone call any time during the meeting. When the call comes, it's up to them to finish the meeting. Brainstorm for five minutes activities they could do. For example, kids could discuss what they've learned so far, contribute a bit of information or advice to everyone, offer a prayer or read a favorite scripture. Appoint one or two people to coordinate and keep things moving.

When the call comes, excuse yourself. Then let the young people continue. Afterward reward them with hero sandwiches and pop. Congratulate them on being heroes and finishing the meeting on their own.

# ✸45✸ Jellybean Jabber

(You'll need a lot of jellybeans in a plastic bag—enough so everyone can have at least a handful. Secure the top of the bag.)

Toss the plastic bag of goodies to someone. Have him or her take as many as he or she wants to eat—but not eat them until you say so. Then have that person toss the bag to another person, who takes as many as he or she wants. Continue until everyone has some jellybeans. Have the last person return the remaining jellybeans to you.

Ask kids to turn to a person sitting close to them. For each jellybean they eat, have kids say one thing they've learned so far in the meeting. If they get stuck, they can start saying things they'd still like to learn.

After everyone has had a chance to eat jellybeans, ask some of the things they've learned so far. When kids respond, toss them another jellybean. Then continue the lesson.

# 46 Chalk It Up to Experience

(You'll need a piece of chalk for each person, water, soap, scrub brushes and a sidewalk.)

Start tossing a piece of chalk to each person. Say: **We've been talking a lot and learning a lot. Now we're going outside to the sidewalk to write or draw things we want to "cement" in our brains.**

Give an example. If you're studying love, kids could draw a big heart and write the words, "Love one another."

Go outside and let the artists design their messages. Take a reading-walking tour around the messages to "cement" them in your memories. Then on with the meeting to learn more.

Have kids scrub the sidewalks after the meeting. Talk about God's "cleansing" power of forgiveness in our lives!

# ⟫47⟪ Over the Net

(You'll need a volleyball net set 4 to 5 feet high and a grassy area or mats.)

Tell teenagers they're going to take a time out to exercise their minds as well as their bodies with a team-cooperation and problem-solving game called Over the Net.

Divide the group into two teams by having kids alternate saying, "time" or "out." All "times" form one group and all "outs" form another. Go to the volleyball net you've set up 4 to 5 feet high. Tell the teams they have five minutes to get one team member over the net without the person touching the ground or the net. They can't use ladders or chairs or other props—just themselves. To make it more difficult, allow no talking.

Afterward, discuss how they solved the problem and how difficult they thought it was. Compare the teamwork to how we support each other through trying times and how we can work to solve problems together.

Wrap up the discussion by saying: **Enough of our time out. Time now to get back to the meeting.**

# Volleyball Variations

(You'll need a volleyball net, ball and other equipment for the variations.)

Gather by the volleyball net and let off steam by playing volleyball. After a few minutes, try one or more of these variations:

● Spread blankets over the net so nobody can see when the ball is coming.

● Play with another type of ball, such as a beach ball, Nerf ball, weather balloon, water balloon, or plastic trash bag filled with balloons or beach balls.

● Add a rule that the ball must bounce before anyone hits it.

● Instead of having kids rotate in their own team, have them rotate back and forth between teams.

● Have kids sit down with their legs crossed and play volleyball with a beach ball.

● Use a balloon and have everyone start on one side. Have the first person who hits the balloon over the net run to the other side, hit it back and remain on that side. Have the next person to hit it over join the other person on the other side. Continue until all players have switched sides.

# ⁂49⁂ Party Break

(You'll need a brown paper bag filled with party surprises such as balloons, streamers, kazoos, party favors and candy. You'll also need punch and punch cups.)

Hold up a brown paper bag filled with surprises. Say: **This is not an ordinary, dull, brown paper bag. It's special on the inside—just like God tells us we are special. God loves our insides as well as our outsides. He knew everything about us even before we were born. Listen to this, then let's celebrate the fact that we're wonderfully made by God.**

Read Psalm 139:13-14: **For you created my inmost being; you knit me together in my mother's womb. I praise you because I am fearfully and wonderfully made; your works are wonderful, I know that full well.**

Let the kids open the bag for an instant party. Blow up the balloons, hang the streamers, pass out the party favors. Talk about how being a Christian is a daily celebration. We have so much to be thankful for because God made us, forgives us and loves us. Form a kazoo band and toot "Onward, Christian Soldiers" or a jazzy rendition of "Jesus Loves Me" and follow the leader as you march.

Serve punch to the kids, and let them sip on it while you continue the program. Occasionally interrupt your meeting with the question, **What do you think about that?**

Let kids toot on their kazoos, "Ta-dah-h-h."

# ⚝50⚝ Balloon Burst

(You'll need a balloon for every two people.)

Form pairs, and give each pair a balloon. If you have an extra person, join in yourself. Have partners stand back to back with their balloon between them. On the count of three, have them squeeze together until they pop their balloons.

Then say, **Now that I have your attention, let's start again where we left off.**

# ⚝51⚝ Balloon Shenanigans

(You'll need a balloon for every two people.)

Form pairs and give each pair a balloon. Have the pairs each place their balloon on the floor. Their first task is to pick up the balloon using only their elbows. Have pairs try it again using only their backs. Run relays with partners placing the balloon between their hips or their heads.

# ⚝52⚝ Paper-Wad Dodge Ball

(You'll need several pieces of scratch paper and a wastebasket.)

Wad up several pieces of scratch paper—

enough so half the kids have a wad. Each time you wad a piece of paper, toss it to someone. Ask the kids without a wad of paper to stand in the center of the room. Ask the kids with a wad to stand around the edge of the room. Say: **We're going to play a version of Dodge Ball. If you're on the outside, throw your paper wads at the inside kids. If you're on the inside try to dodge the wads. If you hit a person below the waist, trade places with that person.**

Keep playing until excess energy has been burned. Place a wastebasket in the center of the room and have kids throw the wadded papers in it. When all paper wads have been thrown away, continue your program.

# 53 Hide 'n' Seek Variations

Say: **Some of you are trying to hide the fact that you wish this meeting were moving a bit faster. We try to hide a lot of facts about ourselves. As Christians, we know we can't hide from God. Let's think more about this truth while we play some variations of Hide 'n' Seek.**

Choose one person to be "It." If you have more than 20 kids, form groups of up to 10. Have each group choose someone to be "It." Have "It" shut his or her eyes and count to 50 while the others hide together—under the stairs, in a closet, behind the choir robes. When "It" finishes counting, have him or her search for the clump of kids.

Another variation is to have one person hide and the others search. When people find the hider, have them hide there also. Have kids continue until everyone is hiding and one person is searching.

When the last person finds the group and you're all bunched up, say: **We know that God seeks us out and chooses us to be his children. He loves us no matter what. So there's no reason to hide.**

Lead everyone back to the meeting.

# 54 Yellow Pages

(You'll need a marker and a piece of yellow paper for every two people.)

Tell the young people to create Yellow Pages ads that will make people want to visit your church. Distribute markers and yellow paper. Have kids work in pairs to design their ads. Encourage kids to describe their church's best qualities and activities using an acrostic. For example, for Hope Church, they could write:

**H**oly place of worship;

**O**ut-of-the-ordinary, fun congregation;

**P**rayer-filled, positive people; and

**E**veryone welcome

Come and see us on Sunday at 8 or 10:30 a.m. for worship and 9:15 a.m. for Sunday school!

Combine the Yellow Pages to display on the church bulletin board. Use the ideas to create an ad for your newspaper.

# 55 Dear Leader

(You'll need a piece of paper and a pencil for every two people.)

Read aloud the following letter to the kids:

> Dear Leader,
>   I'm a student in this class. I'm having trouble focusing on this meeting. Do you have some advice for me to get my attention on the topic?
>                 Signed,
>                 Attention Wandering

Give each pair a piece of paper and a pencil, and have them each write advice to Attention Wandering. Read some of the responses. Encourage kids to follow the sound advice, then go on with your program.

# 56 Bag a Riddle

(You'll need a small brown bag and a pencil for every two people. You'll also need a Bible.)

Say, **Let's bag our meeting for a while so we can bag some stuff.**

Give a small brown bag and a pencil to every two people. Tell pairs each to search the area and find an object such as a pen, pencil or rock to place inside. On the outside of the bag, have them write statements that'll help others guess what's in the bag. Here's an example for a rock:

I'm hard, but I still can be broken.
I can be used for building houses.
You never want to throw me at people.
What am I?

Let everyone guess the riddles. Have a sack of your own prepared. Put a Bible in it. On the outside write:

I'm a best seller.
I'm full of wonderful stories.
People don't read me as much as they should.

What am I?

After kids guess a Bible say, **Let's go on with the meeting to learn more and read more of the Bible.**

# Talk Trippers

Say, **And now I'm going to give you a test.**

Wait for the shocked expressions and conversation to stop, then continue: **I'm not really going to give you a test. I just wanted you to experience a statement that's a definite talk tripper.**

**Let's take a few minutes for pairs to think of talk trippers—statements or questions that would surely stop the conversation if people heard them. For example, the conversation would stop if one night at supper you asked, "Dad, did you ever tell Mom about that bill that came in the mail?"**

Let kids each pair up with a person sitting close to them to create talk trippers. Let pairs tell their trippers to the large group.

Get back to the meeting with this talk tripper: **Time to get back to what we were doing. You'll be graded on how well you listen.**

Pause.

Say, **Just kidding.**

# 58 Follow Me

(You'll need a 10-foot sheet of newsprint, markers and tape.)

Say: **Stop and follow me. No talking.**

Unroll a 10-foot-long strip of newsprint. Title the banner, "Reasons to Follow Us to Church." Give kids markers and ask them to trace their feet. On the feet have them each write one or two reasons they think a person should follow them to church; for example, "Our church is full of friendly, caring people."

Follow the leader, carry the banner and hang it in a prominent place in your church. Then follow the leader back to your meeting area to continue.

# 🌟59🌟 Tic-Tac-Toe Show

(You'll need nine pillows.)

Set up Tic-Tac-Toe on the floor with nine pillows in rows of three. Play guys (X's) against girls (O's). Have an X sit on a pillow, then an O on another pillow, and so on with each trying to line up three in a row. Have teams put their heads together to strategize their moves.

If you have more kids, use more pillows for more Tic-Tac-Toes. Or play more than once so everyone gets a chance.

# 60 Guess Whose Shoe?

Have all kids sit on the floor in a circle with legs crisscrossed and jumbled in the center. Point to a shoe in the jumbled mass of legs, and let someone guess who the shoe belongs to. Have the real owner of the shoe identify himself or herself by trying to untangle. Have the guesser then point to another shoe and have someone else guess its owner. Have kids stay in the circle and continue the guessing.

Vary the activity by having kids lie on their stomachs in a circle with their arms in the center. Have them crisscross and jumble their arms. Then have them try guessing whose hand is whose. "Give a hand" to the best guesser.

# 61 Number Exchange

Say: **Stop! Let's run off some built-up energy. Put your chairs in a circle.**

Ask one person to be "It," and place his or her chair in the center. Have kids number off consecutively from one on up to your group's total size. Then have "It" call out two numbers (no higher than your group's size). Have the kids with those two numbers run to exchange seats while "It" tries to steal one of their seats. If "It" succeeds, have the "dethroned" person become "It." If "It" fails, have him or her try again by calling out two more numbers.

Play for a while, then continue where you left off.

# 62 Treasure Hunt

(You'll need candy or fruit for a treasure. Place the treasure in a brown paper bag and hide it. You'll also need to hide several clues to lead kids to the treasure. Use the ideas in the "Sample Treasure Hunt Clues" box, or write your own. If your group has more than eight people, make two sets of clues.)

When the kids get restless, say: **What do I have here? Ah. It's a clue to find a treasure— just what we need right now.**

Give the first clue to the group. If you have more than eight people, form two teams and give each team a clue. Have them follow the clues to your "treasure."

Let kids munch on their find while you get back to the meeting.

# Sample Treasure Hunt Clues

Make up clues like these samples to fit your church. Don't include the information in parentheses on the clue cards.

## Clue #1

Are you hungry?
Do you need a break?
Search for the clues
and the treasure'll
   taste great.
Look for the next clue
as soon as you can,
by the sugar and salt
and the jar of jam.

*(Hide the next clue
in the kitchen
cupboard.)*

## Clue #2

So you found me.
Aren't you just fine?
Look for the next clue
by a white fine line.

*(Draw a line on a chalk-
board and tape the
next clue by it.)*

## Clue #3

Good job, detectives.
You're really great.
Look for the next clue
by the latch on a gate.

*(Place the clue by the
fence gate.)*

## Clue #4

One more clue is
by a row of seats,
there you'll find
a tasty treasure to eat.

*(Hide the treasure under
one of the kid's seats in
the meeting room.)*

# ✸63✸ Construction Paper Stand

(You'll need a piece of construction paper for every two people.)

Tell the kids: **I've always wanted to see if someone could solve this problem. It's not impossible, but you have to think about it. Two people must stand on a piece of construction paper without touching each other. If you just lay the construction paper down and stand on it, you'll touch your partner quite easily. How can you solve this problem?**

Give one piece of construction paper to every two people and let them try it. If nobody solves the problem, offer the solution: (Lay the paper flat in a doorway. Close the door with one partner standing on the paper on each side of the door.) Kids may discover other solutions as well.

# ✸64✸ Couch Crunch

(You'll need a couch—or an overstuffed chair for a small group.)

Sit on the couch and say, **I've always wondered how many people can fit on this couch.**

Then call someone's name, and have that person sit down beside you. Have that person then call out another name. Keep going, and let everyone try to squeeze in. Stop when there's groaning, so nobody gets hurt!

Say, **So that's how many fit.**

Then get back to your meeting.

# ✷65✷ Look to the Future

(You'll need a big pair of sunglasses like clowns use—or a wild, colorful pair.)

Put on the sunglasses and say: **We're going to take a few moments to look to the future. Each one of us will get a chance to put on the glasses and complete this sentence: "This next week I'm looking forward to . . ."**

After everyone has shared, have kids use their fingers to make eyeglasses and say to a person sitting close to them, "One good thing I see for your future is . . ." For example, "One good thing I see for your future is happiness, because you smile so much and make others feel happy."

Put on the sunglasses again and say, **I see it's time to get back to our meeting.**

# ✷66✷ Sin Stomp

(You'll need five small objects, such as pieces of paper, shoes or whatever's handy.)

Place your five objects around the room. Tell kids the objects represent sin. Have them mingle around the room mumbling, "Sin, sin, sin." When you shout, "Stomp," kids have to run and stomp on the nearest "sin" (or object). The last one to stomp on a sin is out. Have that person help you shout. Continue until only one person is left stomping on sin. Dub him or her the "Senior Sin Stomper," and have him or her lead the others back to their seats.

# 67 Hidden Sin

(Write the word "Sin" on a 3x5 card. Fold it into a tiny square.)

Have kids sit in a circle on the floor with their knees drawn to their chests. Have kids practice passing the folded 3x5 card under their knees. Ask one person to be "It" and stand in the middle with his or her eyes closed.

Have kids in the circle pass the card under their knees. Have all the kids *pretend* they're passing the card around if they don't have it. After a few seconds, have everyone start chanting, "Sin, sin, sin . . ." When "It" hears them chanting, have "It" open his or her eyes and try to guess where the "Sin" card is. Have "It" tag the person he or she thinks has the "Sin" card.

Let several people try being "It." Afterward discuss how it's difficult to hide sin in our lives. Tell kids that rather than hiding sin, it's best to wipe it out with God's forgiveness and grace.

# 68 Rope Jump

(You'll need one long rope and a clear floor space.)

Have kids follow you to the clear area. Stand in the center, hold the rope by one end and start swinging it in a circle close to the ground. Have kids scatter around the room and try to jump over the rope on each revolution.

If a person misses, have him or her take

over and swing the rope. Let a lot of people take turns swinging. Get back to where you left off by saying: **Are you ready to jump back to the meeting? Let's go!**

Part 3

# Race 'n' Relay Boredom Busters

# ⚛69⚛ Search and Find

(You'll need a penny and a Bible.)

Before your program, hide a penny in plain sight (yet not too obvious). When kids are getting antsy, say: **Stand up and search the room. Find an object that's small, flat, solid and round. Don't let anyone know when you've found it; come to me and whisper what it is. If you're right, I'll nod. Then you'll shout, "I see the light!" and stand by me to help when others think they've found it.**

After everyone has found the coin, read Luke 15:8-10 about the woman who loses one coin and searches carefully until she finds it.

# ⚛70⚛ A Meeting Message

(You'll need chalk and a chalkboard.)

Divide the class in half. Give one person on each team a piece of chalk. On a chalkboard, have each team write a message that has to do with what they just learned. The teams can't talk or write notes.

Have the first person write the first word of the message; for example, "We," and then have him or her hand the chalk to the next person who should then write a word; for example, "learned." Have both teams continue until everyone has contributed.

Explain that nobody knows what the message will end up being. The message grows and grows until the last person on each side is given the piece of chalk. These people end their team's message.

Award a rousing hand of applause to the team whose message makes the most sense.

# ⟨71⟩ Pyramid Parade

(Be sure to do this activity on a carpeted area or outside on the grass to avoid possible injuries.)

Announce a pyramid-building race. Divide the class into teams of no more than six. Say: **Each team has 20 seconds to form the tallest pyramid. The team with the tallest pyramid must shout, "We're number one!"**

After kids have formed their pyramids, challenge them to take a step forward—as a pyramid.

# 72 Body Letters and Numbers

(You'll need to meet on a carpeted or grassy area.)

Divide the group in half and see which team can form a number or letter first. Every team member needs to be involved to form the number or letter. Kids can lie down and connect hands and ankles—anything to form what's asked.

Try a few letters and numbers. For example, have kids form A, O, and K. Then say, **You kids are a-okay.**

As a final formation, have the whole group form a one. Shout together, **We're number one!**

# 73 Snake Shake

Split the group in half. Have teams each line up, one person behind the other. Have kids form a long "snake" by placing their hands on the shoulders of the person in front. Then have the first person in each line be the head, the last person be the tail. Say that the object is for the head to grab the other snake's tail. Yell, **Ready, Snake, Go!**

And watch the squirms begin.

# 74 Tag Time

(You'll need a large game room or an outdoor field, and finger foods for refreshments.)

Get everyone's attention by shouting, **It's tag time.**

Call a person's name and have him or her come up and hook one little finger with your little finger. When that person does so, he or she then calls another person up to hook fingers. Continue until everyone's in a straight line with fingers hooked.

Lead the line to the game room or field. Ask everyone to "unhook." Then choose one person to be "It." Tell kids you're going to play Pinkie Tag. On "go," have "It" chase everyone. Others are safe only if they've hooked little fingers with a partner. They can remain hooked for only three seconds, then they have to let go and find another partner.

When kids have let off some steam, have the last person who was "It" lead the others back to the meeting area—single file, little fingers hooked.

Serve finger foods for snacks, such as chips, sandwiches or popcorn.

# 75 Blanket Relay

(You'll need two blankets and two paper fans. Make the fans by folding two 8 1/2x11 pieces of paper like an accordion.)

Say: **Some of you may wish you were taking a nap right now. I'll give several of you a chance to lie down and rest for a while with this game.**

Form two teams by having all kids whose first names start with A through M form one team and all kids whose first names start with N through Z form another team. You may need more teams, depending on your group's size. Mark a line on the floor 30 to 50 feet away.

Spread a blanket on the floor in front of each team. Have the teams each choose one person to lie on their blanket. Give that person a fan. Have all the team members gather around their person, pick up the blanket, and carry the "cargo" to a line and back. The person who's on the blanket should fan himself or herself the whole time. Race several times with other team members taking turns on the blanket fanning themselves.

As a last race, have team members carry their person to the front of the room. Have the first team to finish shout: "Rest and relaxation time's over. On with the meeting."

Another idea is to have the people on the blanket bat a beach ball or balloon up and down the whole time their teammates are carrying them.

# ⚝76⚝ Balloon Bat Obstacle Course

(You'll need a balloon for every two people. Set up an obstacle course. This can be as simple as several chairs kids must run around and a couple of tables they have to crawl under.)

Toss a balloon to a young person and have him or her grab a nearby person to be a partner. Toss a balloon to another person and have him or her grab a person for a partner. Continue tossing out balloons until everyone has a partner and each pair has a balloon. If you have extra kids, you play too!

Tell the partners they're going to run an obstacle course. The trick is the partners must continually bat the balloon back and forth as they run the course. Let kids inflate the balloons and practice batting them back and forth. Then have them run the race. Time the pairs to see who's the fastest.

# Balloon Pop

(You'll need several balloons.)

This activity develops team cooperation and helps kids keep their eyes focused on a goal. Ask kids to count off in twos. All ones are a team, and all twos are a team.

Arrange the teams according to the "Team Lineup" diagram. Have all kids form two lines by facing each other and sitting on the floor with their legs crossed. Put captains at opposite ends of the line.

## Team Lineup

| | |
|---|---|
| 1 (captain) | 2 |
| 2 | 1 |
| 1 | 2 |
| 2 | 1 |
| 1 | 2 |
| 2 | 1 |
| 1 | (captain) 2 |

Toss an inflated balloon in the air above kids' heads. The object is for team members to bat the balloon to their team captain who pops it by sitting on it. Kids can use only one hand to bat the balloon. Their seats must never leave the floor—except to pop the balloon. A team earns a point when its captain pops a balloon.

Try the game several times with several balloons. Then say: **You've kept your eyes on the goal and played a good game of team cooperation. I hate to burst your balloons of excitement, but it's time to go on with the meeting.**

# ⟨78⟩ Tower Builders

(You'll need a Bible, marshmallows and toothpicks.)

Say: **I hear the hum of whispering, babbling voices that reminds me of a Bible story—the tower of Babel in Genesis 11:1-9. You're going to have a chance to see who can build the tallest tower out of the supplies I give you.** Give every two people a handful of marshmallows and several toothpicks. Have a race to see which pair can build the tallest tower—capable of standing by itself—while you read the Bible story. No talking allowed.

Award the leftover tower-building supplies to the tallest-tower builders. Then say: **God scattered the tower builders of Babel throughout all the land. We need to gather for a while to finish our meeting before we scatter on home.**

A variation on this game is to supply a bunch of objects such as boxes and balls. As a group, kids can use those objects and anything else in the room to build one tall tower of Babel.

# 79 Potato Races

(You'll need two metal spoons and two potatoes and enough potato chips for the whole group.)

Point to people one at a time, and assign each person a number as you say this rhyme, **One potato, two potato, three potato, four, five potato, six potato, seven potato, more.** Continue until everyone has a number.

Ask all odd-numbered people to form one team and all even-numbered people to form another team. Set up a line 30 to 50 feet away from the teams.

Give the first person on each team a spoon with a potato on it. On "go," have these people run up to a line and back, balancing the potato. Then have them each pass it on to the next person, who repeats the process. The first team to have all its members run the race wins.

Try these potato-relay variations too:

● Have kids hold the spoons in their mouths and balance the potatoes.

● Have them each hold the potato under their neck. They must run to the line and back, then transfer the potato to the next person's neck without using hands.

● Have them each place the potato between their knees and hop to the line and back.

Ask, **What good things are made from potatoes?**

When someone says potato chips, toss out the bags of potato chips, and let kids munch on the snack while you learn more good things about God.

# 80 Shoestring Race

(Be sure to do this activity in a carpeted or grassy area.)

Say: **You need a stretcher break. I can see some of you itching to move around.**

Form two teams, and have each team line up with one person behind the other. Set up a line 30 to 50 feet away from the teams.

Say: **Everyone grab your shoestrings. If you don't have shoestrings, grab your ankles. Imagine your hands have been smeared with Super Glue, and you're unable to let go.**

Then begin the shoestring-holding relay by having the first one in each line hold his or her shoestrings and run up to the line and back. Each must touch the next person in line, who repeats the process. The first team done wins.

To get "unstuck" from the shoestring-holding positions, play Hip Busters. With kids still holding onto their shoestrings, have them try to knock each other off balance by bumping hips. The last one still holding his or her shoestrings wins. Let the winner lead the others in a few stretches. Then head back to your meeting area.

# ⊰81⊱ Over-and-Under People Relay

Say: **We've gone "over" so much information, you might feel "under" a lot of pressure. Let's make use of this over-and-under feeling by playing an Over-and-Under Relay.**

Form two teams by finding out who prefers steak over shrimp. All those who like steak better, form one team. All who like shrimp better, form the other. Even out teams if necessary.

Have each team form a straight line, standing front to back. Then have the first person stand with his or her legs spread apart; the second person get on his or her hands and knees; the third person stand with his or her legs spread apart; the fourth person on his or her hands and knees; and so on.

Explain that the object of the Over-and-Under Relay is for the team members each to go over and under their teammates. Have the first person in each team begin and go over the person behind him or her, under (between the legs of) the next person, over the next, under the next, and so on. When the person reaches the end of the line, have him or her then assume either a standing or kneeling position, depending on what position the person in front of him or her is in.

When everyone understands, start the relay. Continue until all group members have gone over and under their teammates. Say: **Ready to go "over" some more details with the rest of our** meeting? The relay helped release some tension so you won't feel "under" so much pressure.

# ✵82✵ Stepping Stones

(You'll need four pieces of paper.)

Form two teams by having kids remember the word you say as you point to them. Point to each person, one at a time, as you say either "stepping" or "stone."

All "steppings" form one group; all "stones" form another. Give the first person on each team two pieces of paper. Set up a line 30 to 50 feet from the teams.

One by one, have the team members walk up to a line and back by laying one piece of paper down, stepping on it, laying the other one down, stepping on it, picking up the other, laying it down, and so on. Explain that their feet can never touch the floor—only the paper. If anyone steps on the floor, he or she has to start again. Have each person in the team take a turn. The first team done wins.

Say: **God is our stepping stone in life. No matter what trials or problems we face, we can do it with his help—one step at a time. Let's go back to our meeting and learn more about him.**

# ⟪83⟫ Shoe Win

(You'll need two shoes.)

Form two lines. Give the first person in each line a shoe. On "go," have these people each pass the shoe over their head to the person behind them, who takes the shoe and passes it under his or her legs to the next person. Continue passing over and under until the last person in each line receives the shoe. Then have him or her run to the front and pass the shoe over his or her head to continue the passing. The race continues until all kids in one team are back to their original position.

Declare the winner, then say, **On with the "shoe."**

# ⚡84⚡ Creation Rotation

(You'll need a Bible.)

Take time to read the Creation story and add a little flair. Form two teams. Have each team form a circle, sit down on the floor with kids' legs crossed and their palms up. Ask each circle to choose one person to be a captain.

Say: **Your circle represents the world when it was first created. I'm going to read the Creation story. Each time I read the word "day," your captain slaps the person's hand who's sitting on the left. That person slaps the next person's hand, and so on around the circle until the slap gets back to the captain. Then your whole circle shouts, "And God saw it was good!" I'll keep points on which team finishes first most often.**

Read the Creation story from Genesis 1:1—2:4 and behold how good this activity is at making kids participate!